CU00539944

Introduction

The purpose of this short booklet is to gi[...]
history of Much Hadham. Writing such a bo[...]
First of all there is the paucity of any writter[...]
in our history. Secondly there are times when there is too much recorded history and the problem then is what to leave out. There is already an excellent book on the history of St. Andrew's Church, so I have kept references to the church structure to a minimum. I have tried to make the book a reasonable length without leaving out any important events. I apologise to anyone who feels that I have failed to achieve this target.

The Beginning

The oldest recorded find in Much Hadham was a flint axe from the Neolithic period found a few yards to the west of the ford. There is nothing after that until the Roman period.

The Romans

Britain was conquered by the Romans in A.D. 43 and Colchester became the first capital. From Colchester, Stane Street ran to Godmanchester via Braughing. The section from Colchester to Braughing is believed to have been a Romanised version of a pre-Roman track. Ermine Street running north out of London met Stane Street at Braughing. There were also Roman roads of lesser importance in the area. Among these was a road which left Stane Street at a point about a mile east of Braughing and ran southwards towards the Romano British Temple in Harlow which is now called Templefields. This road entered what is now the north west corner of the parish, passed the area where Carldane Court stands in Bromley Lane, through the gardens of the present Hall, across the ford and up Stansted Hill through Perry Green to Old Park where all traces of it are then lost. The line of the Roman Road can best be traced from an Ordnance Survey map. It is also quite likely that Nether Street in Widford ran further eastward than it does at present and met this old Roman Road.

The Romans remained for about four centuries, and it would seem that they were very active in this area, particularly during the third and fourth centuries. In 1963 a Roman site was discovered just outside the parish covering about sixty acres. Subsequent digging revealed a number of finds including two pottery kilns and a tile kiln, as well as coins and drainage ditches. The pottery found included storage jars, cooking pots, dishes, bowls, beakers and flagons.

The Romans decided to withdraw from Britain and Roman government terminated in 410 A.D.. Thereafter there was a gradual decline and breakdown, accelerated from time to time by the Saxon invaders until, by about 450 A.D., most Roman life had come to an end.

The Saxons

The Saxon settlers had little use for roads. They lived as independent economic units, and they often found that the old Roman roads made useful boundary banks. As a result, even today, some parish boundaries follow the line of old Roman roads. Part of the parish boundary between Little Hadham and Standon is an example. The Tythe Map of 1838 even showed some of the field boundaries as part of the old Roman road.

The withdrawal of the Romans from Britain marked the beginning of the medieval period which ran until about 1500. During this period there were times running for several decades when no records survive, but by using the occasional record and by relating it to what happened in adjacent areas, we are able to get a rough idea of events in Much Hadham.

From about 450 A.D. piratical raids by the Saxons took place followed by more peaceful settlement by them. A Saxon iron dagger with gilt-bronze handle was found in 1938 by workmen digging a ditch at the ford, near to what is now called Sidehill House. The dagger is now in safe-keeping in the Cambridge University Department of Archaeology.

The English conquest by the Saxons was ruthless in its severity and was mainly a conquest by extermination. Then in 596 A.D. Augustine was sent by the Pope to convert the English to Christianity. Christianity grew, and in 596 A.D. Augustine became the first Archbishop of Canterbury.

The Danes

When the Danes invaded England, Alfred the Great, who reigned during the latter part of the 9th century, was able to confine them to the eastern side of England. In this part of the country, the River Lea was roughly the line separating the Saxons and the Danes. Hertford Castle was built as a stronghold from which the Danes could be driven from the country.

Queen Ethelfleda

King Edmund the magnificent was a stalwart supporter of Christianity and framed laws with a view to the reformation of the manners of the clergy and laity. It is at about this time that we have the first written record of Much Hadham. It is found in the will of Queen Ethelfleda, widow of Edmund the Elder, the Saxon King of England from 940 to 946 and a grandson of Alfred the Great. King Edmund was stabbed to death at Gloucester in 946. A.D..

Ethelfleda inherited land at Much Hadham from her father Aelfgar, an Alderman of Essex. She bequeathed this land to her brother-in-law Brithnoth and his wife for use during their lives, and 'after their day' she says in her will 'to Paul's Bury at London to the Bishop's home; and I give to Egwin 'my reeve' (magistrate), 4 hides of land at Much Hadham after my day as it stood in the old days'. Brithnoth's wife, Elfleda, the Queen's sister, also bequeathed her share of the Hadham lands to the Bishops of London. This is the particular event which had the most profound and long lasting effect on the village and which has connected us closely to the Bishops of London for nearly a thousand years.

Carldane Court was also acquired for the bishopric from Eldred, one of Edward the Confessor's Saxon 'thanes', a noble of lower rank than an earl.

It is appropriate to mention here that the name Hadham appears to be of Saxon origin, signifying the home or 'hame' of one, Hadda, but we have no record of him.

William the Conqueror and the Domesday Survey.

Our next record of Hadham comes from the Domesday Survey in 1086 which recorded the owners of land, the nature of its cultivation, and the number and class of the inhabitants. It was both a census roll and a record of estate valuations. In the Domesday Book we see the term 'hundred' used for the first time. No one knows for sure where the term came from, but it is generally accepted that it was, at first, an association of a hundred people for purposes of policing and justice.

Much Hadham was in the Hundred of Edwinstree which was probably in the vicinity of Braughing although there was also a Braughing Hundred. It is not easy to compare the Domesday record with today's boundaries. First of all, it is obvious that a number of mistakes were made when compiling the record. Secondly, it is not always easy to distinguish between Little and Much Hadham. Finally, one of the settlements appears to have straddled what is now the boundary between Widford and Much Hadham Parishes.

Those with a greater interest can read a full translation of Hadham's entry in the Domesday Book, but a rough interpretation from Much Hadham's point of view would probably read as follows:

"The Bishop holds (Much) Hadham himself. It answers for 7½ hides. (A hide is a variable area of land but about enough for one household). Enough land for 22½ ploughs. (A plough is as much land as one plough can work in one day).

Crest of The Bishops of London

In the lordship there are 2 hides, 6 ploughs. A priest, with 35 villagers and one man-at-arms have 15 ploughs. There are 6 smallholders, 2 cottagers, and 12 slaves. One mill, a meadow for ploughing, pasture for the livestock and enough woodland for 200 pigs. This manor is the Bishop of London's.

In Chaldean, Rodhere holds half a hide from the Bishop. There is land for about 2 ploughs, 1 smallholder and 4 slaves. There is woodland to feed 50 pigs, and meadow for one plough. Aldred a thane of King Edward's held this land and was entitled to sell.

In (Much) Hadham, William holds half a hide from the Bishop. There is land for one plough. There is one cottager. Edric, Asgar the constable's man held it and was entitled to sell.

In Leverage, William holds one and a half hides from the Bishop. There is land for 4 ploughs. In lordship 2 ploughs. Three villagers have one plough and there are 2 cottagers and 4 slaves. There is meadow for 2 oxen and pasture for the village livestock. There is wood for fences. Leofwara held this manor from Bishop William. She could sell the half hide but not the other hide without his permission.

In (Much) Hadham, Osbern holds 1 hide from the Bishop. There is land for 2 ploughs. In lordship 1 plough. One villager has half a plough. There are 6 cottagers and 1 slave. Two freemen held this land. One of them Earl Algar's man had half a hide. The other half a hide of the King's jurisdiction. He paid two pence to the sheriff, however, either couple could sell.

The Bishop of London and his men-at-arms hold these 36 hides (in Edwinstree). With them he claims 4 hides which the Abbot of Ely holds in Hadham (probably Little)".

Today the village of Leverage is classed as a deserted medieval village. No one knows exactly where it stood although a map of 1838 has a field on it called Leverage Common. It is assumed that it was somewhere in the vicinity of Minges Farm which is not far from where the old Roman roads probably intersected. There is a Levenage Lane running westward out of Widford which might support that theory.

There are a number of reasons why Chaldean and Leverage should retreat into Much Hadham. In the Hertfordshire Tax Quotas for 1334, there is no mention of either settlement.

As well as ordering the Domesday survey, William the Conqueror also built Waytemore Castle in Bishop's Stortford which had some connection with our local history.

The building of the Church

We now enter a period following on from William the Conqueror where there is little continuation in our history, and we have to piece together the few recorded facts, and assess what happened in between.

We know that the Domesday Book refers to a priest and at sometime the Bishop built a palace to the immediate north of the present church, and it is most probable that a church existed since Saxon times.

Even in those days, taxation was a burden, and at that time taxes were levied both by the crown and by the Pope. Money was required to finance various projects and thus began the process of the church disposing of its assets to raise capital. Part of the grounds where Moor Place now stands, were once the Bishop's ancient deer park and in 1117 the church parted with two thirds of this park to fund a chantry for the repose of the Bishops of London, and mass was to be sung in the lower chapel of the Bishop's Palace. Could our present church have been the chantry which was built from the proceeds of this sale? But our earliest dating of the present church only goes back to about 1220 when the chancel was reconstructed, and a south aisle or chapel was added in about 1240 which was divided from the nave by three arches. About another 20 years later a further two bays were added completing the south aisle to its present length. Then in about 1280 a small transeptal chapel was added to the north east corner of the nave which opened southwards with a single arch. This completed the growth of the church in the thirteenth century.

Henry III visits
In 1248, King Henry III visited the Palace but it is not known why.

Sale of Little Hadham Rectory
In 1276, the rectory of Little Hadham was sold to the Bishops of London by Sir Walter Baud who lived at Hadham Hall. The price was £20. In 1291 an ecclesiastical taxation was made by order of Pope Nicholas IV and the total value of Little Hadham and Much Hadham rectories was set down as £45 - 3s - 4d.

Some early Hadham names
Before we pass into the fourteenth century, it is worth recording some names which have passed down to us. These include a mention in 1287 of John Brand, whose name lives on in Brand's Farm, and in 1294 we read of Geoffrey by Northerne which lives on in North End Cottages.

Edward II 1307 - 1327
In 1307, Edward II came to the throne. During his reign more interesting places in Much Hadham are mentioned. They include: 1307 - 'Emma at Hille'

- Hill Farm; 1307 - 'William Turtel' - Turtle Farm; 1307 - 'John Wynch' - Wynches; 1314 - 'Margary atte Pirie' - Perry Green; 1319 - 'Richard at Melne' - Mill Farm; and 1319 - 'Alice Snellyng' - Snells Cottages.

Our first knowledge of Moor Place also dates back to 1307 when reference is made to 'Daniel ate More'. Later, in the 15th century, the occupier was the grandfather of Sir (Saint) Thomas More.

It should be explained that many of the houses mentioned in early times have been rebuilt, and in some cases, several times since they were first mentioned.

Arms of More of Moor Place

Reginald de Hadham

Although there is no reference to him in local records, there was a Reginald de Hadham who was an influential person connected with Westminster Abbey and who lived to about 1318. He held a number of important posts connected with the abbey and the lands which had been given to the abbey by William the Conqueror, but there was a disagreement over Reginald's election as the Prior to the Abbey during which Abbot Wenlock interfered and the outcome was that Reginald spent a term in the Tower and was excommunicated. However the disagreement subsided and in 1315 an indulgence was issued for all who said a Paternoster and an Ave Maria for Hadham's soul.

Edward III   1327 - 1377

On Edward the Second's death in 1327, his eldest son succeeded him as Edward III, and in this reign it becomes apparent how the interplay between church and state affected our history, and how rectors were selected to accord with the opinions of the incumbent Bishop of London. Edward III's reign lasted exactly 50 years and saw many important events. In 1328, Simon Flambard, our rector was appointed King's Chaplain. He was also a Knight of the Shire. He died in 1331 and was buried in Much Hadham. The oldest monument in the church is a floriated cross engraved on his tomb. At his feet, a lion is inset, and this was originally filled in with brass, which has now disappeared.

In 1346 a list of the principal landowners in the county was prepared. They were assessed in order to levy a subsidy for the purposes of defraying the expenses incurred by the King in the knighthood of his son the Black Prince. The list says that: 'John de Brickendone, holds in Hadham, half a knight's fee; the Bishop of London holds in the same, 'de terra de chaldene', the third part of one knight's fee'. There is also reference to land held by the Bishop of Ely, but that is probably in Little Hadham.

In 1348, the Black Death came ashore in England at Weymouth and eventually worked its way northward passing through Much Hadham. It recurred from time to time in the next three hundred years. The population of the country was reduced by half partly by the plague and partly by a number of exceptionally wet summers during this period. This may have been the time when Leverage ceased to exist and also when Chaldean became integrated into the settlement of Much Hadham.

During Edward the Third's reign we read for the first time of the following places: 1341 - 'Olde Hall', 'Danebridge' and 'Danewood'; 1349 - 'Richard Exenyng' - Exnalls; and in 1369 of John de Ufford' - Uffords and 'Hamstalls' - Homestalls.

Bishop Courtenay
From 1375 to 1380, Courtenay was the Bishop of London. He built the north aisle of the church. His face is still to be seen, looking down on us benignly from one of the corbels in the north aisle which he built. It was Courtenay who called Wycliffe, the reforming priest, to a court at St. Paul's on a charge of heresy in 1377. Wycliffe believed that the ecclesiastical ruler and even the Roman Pontiff may be legitimately corrected by subjects and laymen.

Richard II   1377 - 1399
The son of the Black Prince succeeded to the crown as Richard II in 1377, and in 1380, Courtenay became Archbishop of Canterbury. He was succeeded as Bishop of London by Robert de Braybrooke who built the Church tower and had his coat of arms carved on it. He too was a fiery opponent of Wycliffe. Wycliffe's teachings were probably an unintended contribution to the Peasants' Revolt in 1381. It is possible that by 1388, the first reformers

Private Seal of Bishop Braybrooke

were being confined to the episcopal prison at Bishop's Stortford which Waytemore Castle had now become. The Chaplains in the area had to pay their rent in corn to feed the prisoners.

In 1399 Richard II was deposed. Bishop Braybrooke assented to Richard's deposition in the Parliament House, and signed the document consigning Richard to perpetual banishment. The poor man was to die a year later anyway at the age of 34.

Henry IV   1399 - 1413
Henry of Bolingbroke, fourth son of John of Gaunt, seized the throne from Richard to become Henry IV. Braybrooke carried the Host and officiated at

the coronation. It was a year later in 1400 that the first capital sentence of burning at the stake against a heretic was proclaimed at St Paul's by Roger de Braybrooke. Braybrooke died in 1404 and was succeeded by Roger Walden who died in Much Hadham in 1406.

On a happier note, and of more local interest, we note that Ketwelgrene (Kettle Green) is first recorded in 1404 and Woodside Cottage, (now Sidehill House) is recorded in 1410.

Henry V 1413 - 1422

The House of Lancaster continued with the reign of Henry V in 1413. Henry was the victor at the Battle of Agincourt in 1415 and one of the spoils of war was the hand in marriage of Catherine de Valois, the youngest daughter of the mad king of France, Charles VI.

Catherine and Henry were married in 1420 and their son who was to succeed as Henry VI was born a year later in 1421. Shortly after the birth they were on a tour of France when Henry died. The widowed Queen was given a house in Surrey and had a Welshman, Owen Tudor, as her clerk of the wardrobe. The Duke of Gloucester, regent for Catherine's baby son, admired Catherine, and when he suspected that an affair was taking place between Catherine and Owen Tudor, Bishop Gray the incumbent Bishop of London, made the palace at Much Hadham available to provide a safe place to guard Catherine from Owen Tudor.

At some stage Owen Tudor married Catherine and, as a result, Gloucester passed an Act retrospectively whereby any person marrying a Queen Dowager of England without the consent of Parliament, should be subject to heavy penalties. Owen was imprisoned, but escaped.

Edmund of Hadham

It was at the Palace in Much Hadham that the eldest son of the marriage was born in about 1430. He was called Edmund of Hadham and later Earl of Somerset and also Earl of Richmond. It seems that Catherine and Owen didn't stay in Hadham long because their next child, Jasper, was born at Hatfield, and the third was born at Westminster where he lived as a Benedictine monk.

Catherine died in 1473, overshadowed by the early misfortune of the reign of her eldest son Henry VI, and reproaching herself bitterly for it, in that she consciously disobeyed her husband Henry V's wishes by remaining at Windsor at the time of Henry VI's birth. Henry regarded Windsor as a place of ill-omen for the birth of the heir to the throne. As a punishment to herself, she ordered that the lid of her coffin should be left unfastened so that the curious could gaze upon her face, which they continued to do to the time of Samuel Pepys, who records with glee this satisfaction to his curiosity and who bent down and kissed her embalmed features.

Edmund of Hadham had a successful career. His elder half-brother, Henry VI, gave him precedence over all other English Peers. He married Margaret Beaufort the King's cousin, who bore their son Henry. It was through Margaret's blood that Henry Tudor, afterwards derived his claim to the crown of England as Henry VII.

But Edmund of Hadham died within a year of his marriage so he knew little of his son's life. Margaret was so desolate at her husband's death that she vowed never to marry again, and the vow is preserved in St. John's College, Cambridge, which she herself founded. Nevertheless she went on to marry for a second time, and later for a third time. Her third husband, Sir William Stanley, subsequently placed the crown on her son's head on the field of battle at Bosworth, but was later beheaded by the King for being a traitorous accomplice of Perkin Warbeck a Pretender to the English throne.

Another local name
In 1433, there is the first mention of Warynstenement, now Warrens Farm.

Completion of the Church
In 1456 the church was completed roughly as we know it today, by the addition of the south porch by Bishop Kemp.

Henry VI 1422 - 1471
It was during this reign that the Wars of the Roses were fought between the rival Lancastrian House wearing the red rose and the Yorkists, the white. In 1454, Henry VI was mentally ill, and Richard, Duke of York, had been nominated Protector. Henry's Queen, Margaret of Anjou, revoked the status of the Duke of York. In order to dispute the Queen's actions, Richard journeyed south and made his final camp before approaching London just north of Ware at a place now called King's Hill.

The wars raged for thirty years, with supremacy alternating between the Yorkists and Lancastrians. In 1461, Jasper Tudor led the Lancastrian army for his half brother Henry, and though defeated, made good his escape. His father, Owen Tudor, was captured and beheaded, and Edward, the Duke of York's son, proclaimed himself King Edward IV and started the House of York. This line continued until Richard III was defeated and slain at Bosworth by Henry, Earl of Richmond, to whom had descended the Lancastrian claim to the throne.

Henry VII   1485 - 1509

Thus Henry VII, grandson of Catherine and Owen Tudor, started the House of Tudor which united the Houses of York and Lancaster by Henry's marriage to Elizabeth, the daughter of Edward IV.

The Wars of the Roses probably had little immediate effect on the people of Much Hadham as the mass of the people were indifferent to the struggles, but during the wars the old nobility was practically wiped out, and a larger class of property owners with smaller fortunes replaced the great magnates, and gave rise to the merchant class.

Henry VII reigned until 1509 when he was succeeded by his only surviving son who became Henry VIII.

Henry VIII   1509 - 1547

It is difficult to capture in a few words precisely what occurred in Henry VIII's reign. Though the divorce of Henry VIII from Catherine of Aragon can be described as the occasion of the break with Rome, the Reformation movement had started much earlier. Although Henry claimed the headship of the church, he had no sympathy with the reformed doctrines, and reformers were just as likely to be put to death at the same time as Catholics in support of Papal supremacy.

In 1515, Thomas Patmore became the Rector on the resignation of John Aleyn. Patmore introduced the writings of Luther into his teaching and also consented to the marriage of his curate, Simon Smith, with Joan Benmore and presided at the wedding feast at the Bell Inn, Billingsgate. In 1531, John Stokesley became Bishop of London and whilst concurring in anti-papal measures, he also condemned the Protestants. In 1531 he summoned Patmore with another man, George Bull, who for some unknown reason were both described as drapers, and made them answer for their religious opinions. Patmore was deprived of the living and was succeeded by George Grey as the Rector, but in less than one year, Grey had resigned and was replaced by Thomas Whitehead.

On the dissolution of Religious Houses in 1535, the total value of the rectory, including Little Hadham was £66 - 13 - 4d.

In 1539, 'The Six Articles' became statute. These were popularly called the 'Six Stringed Whip'. They asserted the position of the English Church under six fundamental principles. Failure to believe in transubstantiation - the conversion of the communion wine to blood and bread to the flesh of Christ - was punishable by burning alive, as also was any second offence against the other Articles. In the same year, Bishop Bonner became Bishop of London and soon became notorious. His acts included burning to death a boy aged fifteen.

Edward VI 1547 - 1553

On Henry's death in 1547, his son Edward came to the throne at the age of 10. The Duke of Somerset acted as Protector to the English throne. The Six Articles were repealed and Bonner was imprisoned in The Fleet prison for non-acceptance of Edward VI's injunction and the Book of Homilies. He was released but was soon in trouble again and was imprisoned in Marshalsea for neglecting to use the new Prayer Book. He stayed there till 1553.

Nicholas Ridley was appointed Bishop of London in Bonner's place. Ridley lived at Much Hadham at about this time. There are records of him riding over to Hunsdon to visit the King's eldest daughter Princess Mary. She received him graciously as a friend but indignantly sent him away when he suggested that he might preach to her in the hope of converting her to the Protestant faith.

One of Edward VI's last acts was to order an inventory to be made to find out how much of the church property remained of the plunder of the Reformation era. The Commissioners appointed for Hertfordshire reported that the following furniture was in the church at Much Hadham: a silver gilt chalice weighing eight ounces; two red silk hangings for the altar; five sets of vestments, one of them wrought with Venice gold, the others of red and blue satin; and four copes of chequer work in blue and green. There were five bells in the steeple.

By contrast, in the church at Little Hadham, there was only one silver chalice. All the other furniture had been burned at the previous Christmas, but it isn't known whether this was by accident or design.

Mary I 1553 - 1558

On Edward's death, Ridley denounced Mary and Elizabeth as illegitimate, but he soon perceived that Lady Jane Gray's cause was lost. She only reigned for fourteen days.

Lady Jane Gray was beheaded and was thus safely out of harms way, and Mary came to the throne in 1553. Her husband Philip II of Spain was a devout Catholic and appears to have had a strong influence on Mary's attitude. Ridley flung himself on Queen Mary's mercy but he was deprived of his bishopric. Although Queen Mary declared an amnesty, Ridley was excepted and he was condemned on the capital charge of heresy and burnt alive on 16th October 1555.

Queen Mary restored Bonner as Bishop of London and he set about restoring crucifixes and images and reviving processions. For those who didn't follow his lead there was great persecution. Bonner made great use of the prison adjoining Waytemore Castle where he kept Protestants in a deep and dark dungeon. It was called 'the convicts' prison'. In September 1554, Bonner traversed his diocese and left behind a trail of terror. At Smithfield he had seven people burned alive in one day, and at Colchester, five men and five women on the same day, plus many other single incidents as he traversed through Essex.

The Bishop sent warning of his coming to Much Hadham by means of a mandate dated 25th October 1554. When he arrived at Bishop's Stortford, the rood loft had been decorated and incense was burning and the ringing of bells marked his arrival and departure. He stayed with his niece and her husband for several days in Bishop's Stortford where he was well entertained. He then set out for Much Hadham but as he approached he heard no bells and neither was he met by the Rector Dr Bricket, and he had to send for the key of the church, which he found quite unprepared. The Rector and his supporters pretended that the Bishop was two hours early. The Bishop 'fell to flat madness and raged with a hunting oath or two'. He struck at the Rector with his fist but missed him and instead struck Sir Thomas Jocelyn. It may have been this act which saved the life of the Rector who was clearly a Protestant, because the Bishop refused to stay and took a few of his friends on to Ware. Those left behind enjoyed the meal which had been prepared for the Bishop.

Elizabeth I 1558 - 1603

Before she died in 1558, Mary took steps to ensure that her half sister Elizabeth succeeded to the throne. Knowing of Bonner's reputation, when Elizabeth became Queen she wouldn't let Bonner kiss her hand, but she allowed him to keep his bishopric. But a year later Elizabeth introduced the Oath of Supremacy which all bishops including Bonner refused, and he was committed again to Marshalsea prison where he remained for ten years until his death on 5th September 1569.

In 1561 a list of the principal freeholders in the Hundred included the name of George Haynes of Hadham Magna.

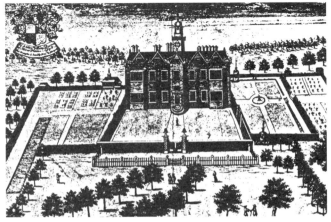

Moor Place – Elizabethan House, demolished and replaced by the present house

Dr Bricket

Bearing in mind the vicissitudes of the previous reign it is surprising that Dr Bricket held the living in Much Hadham until his death in 1562. The living was then granted to Alexander Nowell who achieved much during his 95 years on this earth. He had been made Dean of St. Paul's in 1561 and it was in the next year that he annoyed the Queen. In his efforts to please her, he gave her a New Year gift of a Prayer Book in which he had inserted some pictures representing the Saints. He laid it on her cushion at St. Paul's. The Queen took exception to this saying that it contradicted her Proclamation forbidding the use of images in churches, and that such relics of Popery should be taken away. In spite of this misdemeanour Nowell was subsequently appointed as Rector of Much Hadham.

Bottled beer

Nowell was a keen fisherman and he is mentioned in Isaak Walton's 'The Compleat Angler'. It was while he was fishing in the river Ash at Much Hadham that Nowell accidentally discovered the possibility of bottling beer. He had taken some beer in a bottle when he went fishing and whilst still stoppered he lost it in some long grass. When he returned some days later he found the bottle and was surprised to find the beer still drinkable. The story reached a local brewer who started to sell bottled ale.

But Nowell was also a man of great learning, and he wrote three catechisms. The third, with some modifications, is the one used in the Book of Common Prayer.

After twenty three years as Rector, Nowell was collated to the more valuable first stall at St. Paul's and resigned the living of Much Hadham.

Parish records

As well as the events which were happening related to the church affairs, other things were taking place in the village.

In 1559 we started keeping Parish Records of christenings, marriages and burials and these have been maintained with a few exceptions since then.

In about 1572, a man called Thompson was building the Lordship, and the Newces who at that time were

Family Crest of the Newces

probably the most influential people in Much Hadham apart from the clerics were building The Hall. Martha, daughter of Clement Newce married Lawrence Washington in 1578. Lawrence Washington was the Registrar of the High Court of Chancery, and it was his brother Robert who was a direct ancestor of George Washington, the first President of the United States of America. The Lawrence who lived in Much Hadham would have been a Great-Great-Great-Great Uncle of George Washington.

A year after Martha and Lawrence married, Martha's father, Clement Newce, died. Clement Newce willed that he should be buried in the forenave of the parish church near to his grandfather and father and that a stone be laid upon the grave with a plate fixed thereon engraved with pictures of himself, his wife, and all his children. The stone and brasses are still there.

In 1577 John Aylmer became Bishop of London. He had been a tutor to Lady Jane Gray. He had a hot and fiery temper and pursued a number of causes with vigour. He also subscribed to the Thirty Nine Articles, (The principles under which the Church of England operates). In 1589 he appointed his son Theophilus as Rector. John Aylmer died in 1594 still holding the See and presumably his widow remained in Much Hadham with her son. When she died in 1618, a wall monument was erected in her memory in the south east corner of the chancel.

On 14th September 1578, Queen Elizabeth visited Hadham Hall, in Little Hadham, and held a Privy Council, but the matters under discussion were not related to the locality. They related to a riot in Staffordshire, an outbreak of plague in The Fleet, permission for a man called Houghton to return to England from which he had been banished, and the apprehending of 'an obstinate priest' named Dereham.

James I 1603 - 1625

Five years later in 1603, the year that James I succeeded to the throne, Much Hadham was visited by the plague. Between August and December, thirty deaths occurred from plague in the village. Burials are entered with either the significant letter P or the word Plague and Pest added. In the Goodson's house six people died. So did the landlord of 'The George' which was somewhere close to the Lordship.

In 1610, Nicholas Brett who owned Wynches died. He left a will which is very descriptive of life at the time. The first item he left to his wife was their bed, but he also left his bees and hives to her. He made his son Edward his heir, and he put what was probably Much Hadham's first Tree Preservation Order on some trees which he left to his son George, because he ordered Edward not to 'fell any tree or trees after my decease upon any lands given to George my son before the time of George's entrance'.

1610 was also the birth date of Arthur Capel of Little Hadham. This is significant because the antagonism between the Papists and Reformers now becomes secondary to the divisions between the Royalists and the

Parliamentarians. Arthur Capel became a Royalist leader and in 1641 was created first Baron Capel of Hadham.

It is difficult to follow the progress of rectors at Much Hadham during this period. We know that Peter Hansted succeeded Theophilus Aylmer in about 1620. He too was a Royalist and was appointed Chaplain to Spencer, Earl of Northumberland. He was a poet and dramatist and died in 1641whilst besieged in Banbury Castle during the Civil War.

Charles I 1625 - 1649

Hansted was followed by Thomas Paske, another Royalist, but he was ejected by Parliament in 1643. It was probably during Paske's rectorship that an iconoclastic raid took place on the church. John Skingle from Much Hadham promised money to Richard Mose, Matthew Osborne and George Thorowgood to break down the chancel rails and smash the stained glass windows. This they did, as well as knocking off the head off Lady Aylmer. She still stands there headless. They also burnt the rood loft and damaged other items.

It was also at this time that Richard Haynes and his wife Susan were harbouring homeless people in a barn which was part of the Minges Farm. We shall never know whether they were looking after the homeless people as an act of Christian charity or whether they were harbouring a band of

Minges Farm

© Hertfordshire County Records Office

vagabonds. Richard Haynes was first 'presented' at the Session Court 'for being a harbourer of rogues and vagabonds' and was bound over to appear before Arthur Capel at the next Sessions. His crime was that he 'harboured as many as three score vagrant persons to the terror of those thereabouts. The neighbours thereabouts not daring to assist the constables in apprehending them and saying that when efforts were made to arrest them they crossed over to the adjacent parishes of Sawbridgeworth, Gilston, Widford or Thorley'. But not all the evidence points to the inhabitants as being rogues. The parish register of the time may indicate another point of view. Between December 1639 and February 1642, six people died in this settlement, and two were born and baptised during the year that Haynes provided shelter at Minges. Strenuous efforts were made to deal with the vagrant problem in Much Hadham. During the period that Haynes was offering his hospitality, a total of fourteen search warrants for stolen goods were issued by the magistrates at Hertford, and of these, ten were for Much Hadham, mainly at the request of William Newce.

One wonders from this next extract from the Registers whether poor people made their way to the Haynes' settlement seeking succour. It reads: 'March 17th, 1639, John Anderson, the sonne of Richard Anderson, of Dunstable-houlton, in the county of Beddford, sive-maker, and Sarah his wife, beinge vagrants or poore people, was borne in the Church Porch upon the 9th day of March, in the night tyme, and baptized the day above written.'

In 1643 Paske was ejected from the rectorship, and the living was given first, to the puritan Humphrey Hardewick, and then to Cromwell's own chaplain Daniel Dyke, a Baptist. Meanwhile Baron Capel of Hadham was attending Charles I. His estates were confiscated in 1643 by the Parliament. He aided Charles' escape from Hampton Court and then joined the insurgents in 1648. He was captured at Colchester, but escaped from imprisonment in the Tower. He was re-arrested, condemned by Parliament, and beheaded in 1649.

On 9th October 1646 an ordinance was enacted whereby all property of the bishops was to be sold for the benefit of the Commonwealth. The manor of the rectory was sold to William Collins and Robert Staunton for £899 - 0 - 5d.

Commonwealth declared 19th May 1649

After the Parliamentarians had beheaded Charles I in 1649, and the Commonwealth had been declared, an Act of Parliament was passed which forbad weddings in accordance with the church service and substituted a service before witnesses. These are recorded in our parish registers.

Charles II 1660 - 1685

The Commonwealth, and Cromwell's Protectorate ran its course until in 1660, Charles II - The Merry Monarch - was restored to the throne, and in the same year he restored Paske, who had been ejected seventeen years earlier, to the rectory. Daniel Dyke spent the rest of his days as co-pastor at the congregation of Baptists in Devonshire Square, London.

Perhaps the Merry Monarch's activities were too contagious, because in 1664 the residents of Much Hadham petitioned to reduce the number of inns from 12, to 2 inns and 2 victualling houses because 'the poor people spend their livelihoods in these houses and leave their charges to penury'. The petition eventually had some effect because in 1678 the licence to the King's Head, now Morris Cottage, was given up, leaving the pride of place to The White Lion which stood on the site of the Manor House.

It was in this year that William Stanley became curate at Much Hadham and chaplain to Arthur Capel, the Earl of Essex. Arthur Capel was the eldest son of the first Baron Hadham. He fought in the King's army and and was created Earl of Essex in 1661. He opposed both Charles II's efforts to obtain arbitrary powers, and his leaning towards Catholicism, and associated himself with Monmouth's schemes to overthrow Charles which led to the Rye House plot which took place in 1683.

The responsibility for maintaining the highway fell to the parishes. Many parishes felt that this was an unfair burden and this led to turnpike roads where travellers had to pay a contribution towards maintenance costs. One of the first turnpikes was at Wadesmill. Although there was a break in collecting tolls at Wadesmill from 1680 to 1690, the road through Much Hadham was still the most frequently favoured route.

King Charles and the Duke of York had been to the racing at Newmarket Heath and a fire had broken out which caused them to return to London a week early. Their route would have taken them through Saffron Walden, Much Hadham and Hoddesdon. The Earl of Essex with a number of Whig supporters attempted to murder the King and the Duke of York as they passed through Rye House. They were arrested and sent to the Tower. The Earl of Essex was found in his cell with his throat cut, and it has never been determined whether or not this took place by his own hand.

Feelings between the Papal supporters and Protestants were still running high, and in 1679 an order commanding the Constable of Much Hadham was given to deliver a list of recusants - those who refused to attend the services of the Church of England - to the justices of Hertford. The order was returned by the constable endorsed 'certified that I have no Popish recusants in the Parish'.

The Earl of Essex had presented William Stanley to the rectory of Rayne

Parva in 1681, but Stanley avoided taking up this appointment.

The Bishop of London held a conference in Much Hadham in 1684. The vicar of Bishop's Stortford, Thomas Leigh B.D., preached the sermon on 'The keeping of Holy Days'.

Charles II's reign lasted until 1685. Thirteen of his mistresses are known by name. Presumably to be on the safe side in the afterlife, he declared himself a Catholic just before he died.

James II 1685 - 1688

John Goodman had been Rector since 1674, and was still in Much Hadham when James II came to the throne on Charles' death. William Stanley was Goodman's curate. In 1685 Stanley was appointed as chaplain to the Princess of Orange.

William III 1689 - 1702

James fled the country in 1688 and after a short interregnum William III succeeded to the throne.

Mary II 1689 - 1694

Mary became Queen of England in 1689. In the same year, the Act of Toleration became law, by which religious freedom (denied by the Act of Uniformity and the Five Mile Act) was granted to all dissenters from the Established church except Catholics and Unitarians.

In the same year Stanley became Clerk to the Closet. Then in 1690 when John Goodman died, Stanley became Rector. There is a memorial marble to John Goodman in the church.

Stanley was renowned for his stentorian voice. He became the Dean of St. Asaph's (North Wales) in 1706 but retained the rectorship of Much Hadham. He married Mary, the daughter of Sir Francis Pemberton, Lord Chief Justice of England and had three sons, Thomas, William and Francis.

Anne 1702 - 1714

Queen Anne's reign from 1702 to 1714 seems to have passed by Much Hadham largely unnoticed with Stanley still the Rector.

George I 1714 - 1727

George I's reign which started the House of Hanover also appears to have been relatively quiet, although not entirely without events worth recording.

In 1698 the Society for the Promotion of Christian Knowledge was founded with the aim of establishing charity schools. This movement spread throughout the country and it was probably with the S.P.C.K. in mind that Mary Hales, widowed daughter of Clement Newce willed in 1720 the sum of £700 to the Rector in trust for the poor. She also gave £500 for 'a schoolmaster or schoolmistress to teach 6 poor boys and 6 poor girls to read, write and cast accounts, and, as regards the girls, to sew, knit and spin'.

William Stanley resigned the living in 1723 and his son Francis became Rector.

George II   1727 - 1760
Windmills
In 1728 Nathaniel Salmon wrote a history of Hertfordshire in which he refers to Much Hadham as follows: 'In about 1722 there was a remarkable whirlwind in the street of Much Hadham which lifted up a number of muslins laid upon a hedge to dry. This is an old Hertfordshire custom. It carried some as far eastward as the windmill, and others within half a mile of Bishop's Stortford Town'. By this date there had been at least two windmills in Much Hadham. From the account given by Salmon, this windmill was probably the one standing very near to the site where Walton's Cottages now stand.

The Hall
When Mary Hales died there wasn't enough money to fulfil the wishes in her will and so the Hall which had been her home, had to be sold. The Hall was bought in 1725 by William Stanley who had been the Rector until 1723. When William Stanley died in 1731, his will dated 1729 says 'I give to my son William, after his mother's death, my house in Much Hadham which I lately built'. This gives us a fairly accurate date for the building of the Hall, but the architect is still uncertain. Stanley's close connection with St. Paul's cathedral which was completed in 1710, put him in touch with the best craftsmen of the period and it is believed that John James was probably the architect. The two reasons to support this are first, that James built a similar house for himself at Eversley in Hampshire, and secondly, that he succeeded Wren as Surveyor to the Fabric of St. Paul's after Wren's death in 1723.

Punishments
At this time, each parish was responsible for its own poor and vagrant people. If they left their own parish they were frequently returned by order of the courts. Punishments at the time were also severe and salutary. Here are three examples.

On 2nd April 1733 there was an Order allowing the appeal of Sawbridgeworth against a warrant removing Sarah Hampton, aged 18 months, from Great Hadham. 'The mother, Esther, wife of John Hampton, yeoman, was delivered of the child while she was in Hertford gaol, and has now been transported for robbing her master, Samuel Petchy of Sawbridgeworth'.

On 3rd October 1737, Richard Benfield and William Malin of Great Hadham, labourers, were sentenced to be whipped for stealing 8 pounds of wheaten bread, 5 pounds of cheese and a wooden handled knife from Simon Rouse.

On 26th April 1742, John Everitt and Thomas Randall of Great Hadham, labourers, were sentenced to be openly whipped for stealing three blocks from Mary Stevens, spinster.

Duelling at the White Lion
In 1754 The White Lion (now the Manor House), lost its licence. The story is told that this was on account of a duel fought in the garden, wherein a Member of Parliament was killed. Unfortunately the House of Commons library is unable to confirm this story.

George III 1760 - 1820
The 'Pest House' (Map ref. O.S. 435203) was originally built as an isolation hospital for the village. The date over the door was 1767. The building eventually became part of Lordship Farm and was occupied by farm labourers until 1914. On the O.S. map it is shown as Bushwood Cottage. Its ruins were discernible until the mid 1980s, but all trace of it has now disappeared.

The first bridge
Until 1767, Much Hadham was reached entirely by fording the rivers which surrounded it, but at about that time the first bridge across the Ash was built between Hadham and Widford by the Mill. It was built by William Parker with contributions from parishioners after a man and two horses were drowned in attempting to cross the ford when flooded.

Almshouses
In 1774, the old White Lion (now the Manor House) became an almshouse and was used for vestry meetings.

Anthony Hamilton
In 1775, on the death of Francis Stanley, Anthony Hamilton became Rector. There is a tablet in his memory on the north wall of the church. He remained Rector for 37 years.

Moor Place

Shortly after Hamilton became Rector, James Gordon built Moor Place which replaced an older house which stood near to its present site. James Gordon's coat of arms can be seen above the front door of Moor Place.

Another bridge

It seems that the first bridge at the mill didn't last long because the inhabitants of Much Hadham and the neighbouring villages presented a petition in 1786 complaining of the inconvenience arising from the frequent floods at Hadham Mill for want of a bridge over a river there. A committee of justices was appointed to consider the petition. It reported that it was necessary that a bridge should be built at Hadham Mill. The court accepted the estimate of John Best of Hertford, carpenter, to build the bridge for a sum of £235 - 13s - 5d upon the supervision of John Glyn, surveyor.

Lunatic Asylum

In May 1803 Robert Jacob of Much Hadham, gentleman, was granted a licence to keep an house for the reception of lunatics not exceeding ten in number. Dr Dimsdale was the physician appointed as the visitor and inspector. This was The Palace. It remained a lunatic asylum until 1858. It appears from the occasional list of inmates that they were all titled people or those who had connections with the church.

Thomas Randolph

When the Rev. Anthony Hamilton died in 1812, Thomas Randolph became Rector. His father was the Bishop of London and Thomas became Rector six months after he had taken Holy Orders in 1812 at the age of twenty three. He remained Rector until his death in 1875 having been Rector for 63 years. During his rectorship he undertook a number of projects to enhance the church, including the restoration of the chancel window.

Randolph also created the rectory garden. Many of the seedlings and cuttings came from Lambeth Palace, his father's official residence.

The year after Randolph became Rector he was called to appear before the magistrates to prosecute John Brace 'of Much Hadham, victualler, the master of a public house called The Bull', for permitting a fight to take place on his premises. The evidence was that on Friday evening 22 October 1813 an affray and a fight took place at The Bull between John Dowsett and Daniel Rolph, both of Much Hadham, in consequence of which Rolph lost his life. 'John Brace the master of the public house did not endeavour to prevent the affray but on the contrary the doors of the said public house appeared to have been fastened to prevent the said fight from without'. The outcome is not recorded.

George VI   1820 - 1830
In July 1827 we find our first traffic offence. Charles Wallis of Much Hadham, labourer, was fined fined 4s for careless driving.

William IV   1830 - 1837
In 1834 the school had about 50 scholars of whom 18 were instructed free of charge in respect of Mrs Mary Hales' charity of 1720 and Mr John Somes' charity of 1772.

In May 1835, Mr John Dalyell, was Master of the Puckeridge Hunt. He lived at The Lordship. His first whipper-in and kennel huntsman was John Skinner who came with him from Forfarshire. Mrs Dalyell was the first lady to ride with the Puckeridge hounds. Tradition has it that the hounds were at one time kenneled at the Lordship. The cottages opposite are known as Whiprow Cottages. It is assumed that at that time they housed the hunt servants. Dalyell appears to have been a rather unpopular figure and only stayed until 1838.

In the Autumn of 1836 Henry Warwick, a labourer of Much Hadham was sentenced to 3 months hard labour for assaulting Joseph Speller the parish constable.

The Lordship Stables in 1912

Victoria 1837 - 1901

The parish constable was elected annually and was the executive officer of the parish and was assisted by a watchman. But in 1839 parliament passed The Rural Constabulary Act. Shortly after that we see reference to our first village policeman. Henry Bowfell, Much Hadham's first policeman was summoned to court to give evidence against James Wright. But he doesn't appear to have stayed long because shortly afterwards Charles Hampton, yeoman, and Henry Rutherford, policeman, both of Much Hadham were summoned to court to give evidence against Thomas Cutmore.

In 1843 the report on the lunatic asylum stated that there were 7 males & 6 females. Among the list of names were John Thorpe, husband of the Rt. Hon. Lady Hannah Charlotte Thorpe, admitted 1817; William Thomas Toke, son of the Rev. W. T. Toke; Mary Alston, wife of Rev. V.T. Alston; Mary Ann Colebrook of Bath, sister to Lady E.S. Colebrook.

The Congregational Church

The Little Hadham Congregational Church was established before the one in Much Hadham. The Little Hadham worshippers kept a detailed record of their activities. In 1846 the Rev John Phair wrote: 'Went to Much Hadham to embrace the offer of a building. Hired the place at £5 per annum'. In 1847 they recorded: 'This day, the chapel at Much Hadham was opened for Divine Worship on Sabbath evenings in connection with and under the charge of the Pastor and Church of Congregational Dissenters at Little Hadham. The following year they recorded: 'Anniversary at Great Hadham. Good Attendance. Fine Day. Fair Collections'. Then a year later: 'Anniversary sermons were preached. Collections small. Attendance middling. Two or three causes may be assigned, but not suitable to enter'. It would be nice to know what those reasons were! Then in 1860 the record shows that the Great Hadham Anniversary was postponed 'on account of the floods'.

St Thomas's Church, Perry Green

At the instigation of Richard Hunt, St Thomas' church was built at Perry Green in 1853. It was erected for the convenience of the inhabitants, chiefly farm labourers, of the outlying district as they lived some distance from the parish church, which is nearly two miles from the parish church.

In the same year a skittle alley was added to The Bell public house.

The Ware, Hadham and Buntingford Railway.

The next few years must have been exiting times in the parish because of the spread of railway systems throughout the country. By 1843, a railway line had been opened between Broxbourne and Ware and a few years later a railway running north from Ware was planned but came to nothing. In 1856 a meeting was held to discuss building a railway from Ware or Hertford to Buntingford following the Rib Valley, but one or two landowners were so strongly opposed to the plan that another route had to be found and the idea of running the track up the Ash Valley and then crossing over to Standon and on to Buntingford was conceived. When a company was formed for the project, Richard Nicholson and Richard Hunt of Much Hadham became directors. The company had many teething troubles. There was difficulty in obtaining sufficient finance. Several landowners were opposed to the scheme including the Rev Thomas Randolph, but eventually approval was given by Parliament and work started. About two hundred men were working on the line in the Much Hadham area, and they were lodged in the local inns. Because of financial difficulties, the management of the company was taken over by Eastern Counties Railways in 1862 even before the line was finished. A month later Eastern Counties Railways amalgamated with other companies to become the Great Eastern Railway.

The next year, a few days before the railway was due to open, an accident occurred and a young navvy was killed. The inquest was held in The Bell Inn, (now The Old Bell), and he was buried the following Sunday. On the following Tuesday, 10th Feb 1863, the first train ran taking shareholders from London to Buntingford for the half yearly meeting. This special train ran before the Board of Trade inspection on the 18th April. The line failed the inspector's test and serious criticisms were made regarding safety, but these had been rectified by the time the line made its first scheduled journey on 3rd July 1863.

The line was not a success and by 1865 the directors of the company were in dire straits and they were hoping that the Great Eastern Railway would get them out of trouble. A special meeting was held and Richard Hunt was vehemently opposed to selling out, but the majority of shareholders agreed to make over the Company to the Great Eastern Railway. Richard Hunt then gave up his interest in the railway.

Apart from improved travel, the railway brought other benefits to Much Hadham. The existence of a railway siding meant that coal could be brought in more cheaply and coal dropped in price locally by about five shillings a ton.

Almshouses

The sign over the Almshouses reads: 'Almshouses rebuilt 1866'. There is a story that a photograph of the earlier Almshouses used to hang in the village hall. It was a two storey building. All evidence of the earlier building has been lost.

The recording of Congregational Church activities continued. The record in 1868 includes: 'A desire for a new church was expressed and Mr Richard Hunt gave the site to build one'. The church and schoolroom were completed in 1872. The pastor was the Rev. T M Newnes, son of Sir Thomas Newnes, the founder and publisher of 'Tit-Bits' (a well known weekly magazine of the time).

Several other buildings went up at about this time. The sign over the Flint House gives the date of 1869. It is believed originally to have been the junior school. It was then changed to Flint Cottage before becoming Flint House.

In his history of Hertfordshire in 1872, Cussans refers to Culver Lodge. He describes it as 'an old fashioned brick building which was lately in possession of Henry William Field who was for fifty years the Assay Master of the Mint'. By 1872 it had become a convent, dedicated to the Holy Child Jesus.

The principal landowners in 1872 were Richard Hunt and the rector the Rev Thomas Randolph.

Family Crest of Richard Hunt

On 15 May 1875 the Parish Magazine which in those days was called 'Church Bells' records: 'The Rev Thomas Randolph, Rector of Much Hadham, Little Hadham and Perry Green and prebendary of Cantlowes, died on Saturday at the age of 86. He was a son of Bishop Randolph, and graduated in 1809 at Oxford. He was ordained deacon and afterwards priest in the same year (1812), and when he had only been six months in full orders he received the appointment which he has held for 62 years. The value of his rectories is stated in the clergy list to be £2,036 a year, and that of his stall is supposed to have latterly been not far short of twice that amount'.

Building sites for sale

The arrival of the railway brought development pressure to Much Hadham. Several schemes were implemented which had various degrees of success. Some land comprised small plots on which week-end chalets could be built so that Londoners could get into the country for some clean air. Other schemes were for housing estates for the occupation of commuters. A report from the Herts and Essex Observer of September 1877 reads:

'On Thursday a sale was held of building sites on the Mill Park Estate, Much Hadham, which is situated just off the main London road in the direction of Widford. The estate comprises 80 acres.

About one third of the whole acreage has been divided into 220 plots and these were offered for sale. Some 130 persons from London attended the sale and returned by special train. Luncheon was provided before the sale, which began at 2 o'clock.

In the time at their disposal the auctioneers sold 56 plots for £632 or at an average of £11 per plot. The railway company has decided that as soon as there are 20 season ticket holders to London from Mill Park they will provide an early fast train to London, arriving there between 8 and 9 a.m. and also two extra fast down trains in the evening.

It is one of the stipulations that no house or shop shall be erected fronting Bourne Road and private terrace drive at a less value than £250 each, and on any other part of the estate the value of each house must not be below £200'.

Gunpowder Works

Because the railway was nearby, the Smokeless Powder Company established a 126 acre site at Barwick and built a road across to the station yard so that it could transport cordite, gun cotton, torpedoes, cartridge fuses and on occasions, nitro glycerine and dynamite to Enfield Lock, North Woolwich and other military establishments.

During its life, the bridges of the railway were rebuilt to take heavier locomotives, and changes were made from time to time to the station structure and a station master's house was added.

Gas

By 1880 the Much Hadham Gas Co. was making gas in the village and offered to supply the station with gas for lighting purposes. On 17th March 1887, there was a sale of 20 shares of Much Hadham Gas Co Ltd. They were sold as follows: Five shares each were bought by Mr T W Ashwell and Mrs Millard, and the remaining ten were bought by Mr Joseph Stracey.

Richard Hunt and Windmills

Richard Hunt who lived at Culver had given up his interest in the railway but continued to undertake entrepreneurial investments. He built Uffords Farmhouse and its enormous red brick barn. He also built several other houses including Wheatcroft and Wheatcroft Terrace. In addition to Culver he owned Old Park and Hadham Mill Farm. To maintain these he employed an agent, Mr Frederick Camp.

One of Richard Hunt's strangest ventures was to build the last windmill to be constructed in Hertfordshire. There are records of three windmills in Much Hadham.

The first was approximately 220 yards east of the church. It was shown on a map dated 1676 but had not previously been recorded. It was still shown on maps as late as 1855.

The second was about half a mile north of Much Hadham and was shown

The Windmill

on maps between 1766 and 1850.

The third was the one from which Windmill Way takes its name. It was once described in this way:

'The most unusual windmill we have had in the county once stood at Much Hadham. It had eight sails and a large doorway in the base through which a waggon could be driven for unloading corn. It was built by a Lincolnshire millwright as recently as 1892-93 and was the latest of all the Hertfordshire windmills. Typical of Lincolnshire mills, it had a tall, slender tower and an 'ogee' shaped cap with an automatic fan. There were two balconies round this mill, one half way up (to give access to the sails) and the other at the top where the fan was within reach. If it is true that the sails came off in 1906 as we are told, it can have worked for no more than 13 years - not long enough to have paid for the cost of its building'.

It is true that the windmill worked for only a short period. This was because Richard Hunt who had previously been a director of the railway company had withdrawn after falling out with the other directors. The sails of the windmill protruded over the railway land and the Company was able to force him to remove the sails to avoid this interference. At eight stories high it must have been a prominent landmark. It was struck by lightning shortly after it was built. During the 1914-18 war it was turned into flats for Belgian refugees and as a food store, and afterwards the Much Hadham Brass Band

Yew Tree Farm in about 1910

The Old Post Office – Now Plummers Cottage

© Hertfordshire County Records Office

The Red Lion

under the direction of Mr Roberts used it for band practice until the early 1920's. It was sold for demolition in 1927 but the bricks were so well bonded together that they were unsuitable for re-use.

Norman family buys Moor Place

Moor Place was bought by the Norman family in 1886. Yew Tree House was not part of the estate at that time as it belonged to Richard Hunt who also owned all the land to the south of Kettle Green Lane.

The William Morris family

In the late nineteenth century The Lordship was owned by a Mrs Nicholson. Mrs Morris also lived at The Lordship before and after Mrs Nicholson's death from at least 1888 to 1895 with her daughter Margaret. They were mother and sister of the famous poet, artist, socialist and founder of the Kelmscott Press. Mrs Morris eventually moved to Morris Cottage and stayed there until her death.

Morris Cottage formerly The Kings Head

County Council created

The Local Government Act of 1888 created County Councils. Before this the business of the county was administered by the Justices in Quarter Sessions. The newly formed County Councils also took over from the old Highway Authorities.

Hodge's Garage was also established in 1888.

The Police House

On 22nd October 1894 the Finance Committee of the County Council debated the possibility of building a police house in Much Hadham. Land had been purchased from Mrs A S Mott and others for the sum of £78 - 10s and the land tax of £2 - 12s - 1d had been redeemed. There was some opposition to the proposal. It was suggested that the parishes of Great and Little Munden had a more urgent need. Mr T F Halsey, supporting the idea, said that the proposed police station at Hadham merely meant the erection of a Police Constable's residence with a place where a man could be locked up for a day or so, because Much Hadham was a petty sessional division. A sergeant would reside in the house which would consist of six rooms and a lock up and he would pay 3s 6d a week.

District and Parish Councils created.

The Local Government Act 1894 created District and Parish Councils. The first Parish Council meeting in Much Hadham was held in December. There were ten councillors and the chairman was Mr W J Hart. The District Council was the Hadham Rural District Council, which included Thorley, Sawbridgeworth and Braughing.

Some of the issues which the District Council discussed in its first full year (1895) were:

- where the council should meet;
- approval of a planning application to build two cottages for Mr R Hunt near Exnalls - now called Exnalls Cottages - and comments that the cottages were being erected before the plans were approved. The Clerk was instructed to write and tell him in future to get plans passed before commencing work;
- a letter from Rev. Stanley Leathes regarding putting Whip Row Cottages on mains drainage and other Plans for 8 cottages Near Culver Lodge passed for Mr R Hunt.

In the following year (1896) other interesting items appear in the minutes including:

- Planning approval for a farmhouse for Mr R Hunt. This is now Uffords.
- Proposals for Hadham and Stansted Rural District Councils to acquire land at Bishop's Stortford to build an isolation hospital on the site of the Bishop's Stortford Union.
- planning approval for the Rev. Leathes to convert the pigeon house at Rectory Lane into a dwelling house.
- planning approval to build a public house at Hadham Cross for McMullen and Co. This is now The Old Crown.
- Authority to water the streets in Much Hadham to keep the dust down. Although approved this was not taken up immediately as it was regarded as being too expensive.

Disease and pure drinking water

In the following year there were 10 cases of scarlet fever at Green Tye and one in the village. This appears to have generated a great deal of discussion regarding the provision of pure drinking water and the disposal of sewage. It probably also led to the idea of watering the streets. There appears to have

The High Street facing North

© Hertfordshire County Records Office

Inscription inside entrance to Hadham Towers

© Bill Trigg

The High Street facing South from The Bull Inn

© Hertfordshire County Records Office

View of Hadham Towers from Hadham Hill

© Bill Trigg

been a considerable division of opinion between those who sought to improve matters and those who rejected any idea of change, mainly on the grounds of expense.

In July 1897, Hadham R.D.C. were told that two cottages at Woodside (now Sidehill House), the property of Admiral Randolph were without a proper water supply. The Clerk was told to communicate with the agent Mr Gayton.

In due course a water van was bought to water the streets at a cost of £40 - 19 - 0.

A short time later authority was given to connect the school water closets to mains drains. Mr G L Thurgood undertook the work.

In November a child at the children's home contracted scarlet fever and was moved to hospital. Subsequently, the District Council received a report regarding the water supply which said that:

'There are 60 houses at Hadham Cross dependent on water supply from shallow wells, and there are about 120 houses between Hadham and Lordship Farm in a similar state'.

In January 1898 scarlet fever was still in the district. The schools were disinfected but the Managers of the schools complained about the damage done to the schools by the disinfectant.

On 17th February 1898 approval was given to send a final notice to supply water to Woodside Cottages. The Council then turned its attention to two cottages belonging to Mrs Hunt 'situate near the station' which were without water supply.

In September a letter was received from an Inspector urging the council to improve the water supply and so a Parish Meeting was called in October. The response from the Public Meeting was 'that the village is of the opinion that the village, as a whole, is well supplied with water and that there is no present necessity of incurring the extra expense of a water scheme.'

But sickness was still rife in the village. In June 1899 there were two cases of scarlet fever in Maltings Lane (as it was then called), and two cases of scarlet fever and two of diphtheria at the children's home. One of the children was prematurely discharged from the hospital. Miss Symes of the children's home attended the District Council meeting and complained about the condition of the child on its discharge. Apparently Mr. Norman took the matter up and incurred the displeasure of the District Council. The Council received the following letter from the Local Government Board:

"I am directed by the Local Government Board to forward to the Hadham R.D.C. the accompanying extracts from a letter which the Board have received from Mr F H Norman of Moor Place together with a copy of of an enclosure referred to therein respecting certain cases of scarlet fever at the children's home in Much Hadham and I am to request that the Board may be furnished with the observations of the R.D.C. upon the allegations in her letter of the Misses F Symes and L B Hoshier.(1) that a patient who had been in association with cases of scarlet fever and had been in the isolation hospital was sent home while her skin was still freely peeling, and(2) that letters, books, and unmarked linen which had been in use or in possession of patients in the isolation hospital were sent home with them" The District Council discussed the letter and then passed the following motion: 'That this Council regrets that Mr Norman, during his year of office as High Sheriff of Hertfordshire should have, as a resident in Hadham, written to the Local Government Board regarding the Hadham R.D.C.'s action without first communicating with that body'.

This is one of the many instances where the Norman family have concerned themselves with the welfare of the villagers during their ownership of Moor Place.

By the turn of the century the County Council had also become concerned and passed a resolution that the Much Hadham water supply was inadequate. But the Parish Council were not prepared to act as it would mean a charge on the rates.

In February 1900 the District Council first discussed the Housing of the Working Classes Act 1890. Reference was also made to the Elementary Education (Defective and Epileptic Children) Act 1899. It may be that the Councillors were aware that His Eminence Cardinal Herbert Vaughan had already written to the Superior General of the Daughters of the Cross of Liège asking for the sisters to start a residential school for children suffering from epilepsy.

Dame Clara Butt

At about this time Mr. and Mrs Hastings Wilson lived at Hadham Mill. Beryl Knight, when reminiscing about Much Hadham, wrote 'I remember Dame Clara Butt well. About 50 years ago, she and her husband Mr Kennedy Rumford used to stay at Hadham Mill. Charity concerts were often arranged at the village hall, which usually filled up during the afternoon in readiness for the evening performance, and Hadham Street would be crowded with carriages of all shapes and sizes to say nothing of traps, pony carts and gigs. Seats were priced as low as 3d and 6d. Dame Clara Butt singing "Abide with me" would be a great moving experience of the evening.'

In June 1900 Sawbridgeworth and High Wych were separated from Hadham R.D.C. to become Sawbridgeworth Urban District Council.

Gilebe Cottage

© Hertfordshire County Records Office

View of Plummers Cottage

© Hertfordshire County Records Office

Later in the year M.H. Parish Council agreed to formulate a scheme for improving the water supply provided they could be authorised to consult an expert to be paid for by the District Council.

Queen Victoria died at the beginning of 1901.

Edward VII 1901-1910.

© Bill Trigg

Hadham Towers

The house called Hadham Towers was built in 1901 by Charles Fitzroy Doll who lived from 1851 to 1929. He was an architect and was surveyor to the Duke of Bedford and his estate. Doll built the Russell Hotel in 1898 which was described as "a frenzy of terracotta". He also designed many other outstanding London buildings of the time. His father was German and for 52 years was Page of the Presence to William IV and Queen Victoria. Doll served for some years on Holborn Borough Council and was twice Mayor. Inside the porch of Hadham Towers was a beautiful dedicatory inscription, painted for the opening of the house in 1901 which showed that Doll had a sensitive Arts and Crafts personality concealed within him.

St. Elizabeth's School and Home

On 6th February 1902 the Council approved plans for a school and house for epileptic girls at South End for the Daughters of the Cross of Carshalton, Surrey. This is Saint Elizabeth's School and Home. A cottage had been bought for £200 and land at £2-2-0 an acre, bringing the total purchase price to £1,253.

The water works

In April 1903 Messrs Pollard and Tingle were appointed as engineers to the water scheme. They were instructed to acquire land, to sink a borehole and to build a reservoir. The solicitors were Gayton and Hare. Their task wasn't easy. They had to prepare for a Public Enquiry and make arrangements for a loan. Mr F H Norman suggested that the details should be printed for the benefit of parishioners.

By May 1905 draft specifications for tenders for a reservoir, a cottage and mains piping were ready.

Sickness was still rife in the village. In June 1905 there were four cases of scarlet fever all in the same family one of whom died.

The work on the water-works scheme was completed by the end of the year and in January 1906 Mr. Thurley commenced his duties as the caretaker and maintenance engineer. The waterworks were at the top of Bromley Lane.

The work in laying the pipes caused considerable discontent with claims for compensation and complaints about the re-instatement of the areas where the pipes had been laid.

By July 1906 water had been laid on to thirty six houses in Perry Green, Green Tye and South End. Water had also been laid on to two houses at Hadham Cross. The Parish Council was encouraging various public houses and Perry Green and Much Hadham Schools to connect up to the system which they did by the end of the year. No sooner had this been done than the Herts and Essex Waterworks Co. served an order on the Parish Council saying that it intended extending its supply to Thorley, Great Hadham, and Little Hadham and stating that it wished to take over the existing supply at Much Hadham. The Council agreed to confer.

Telephones

In May 1908 the Council received a letter from the Ware office of The National Telephone Co. saying that it was about to connect Hadham with the main telephone system and suggesting that the village should be connected with the water works. The Council decided not to respond.

In May 1909 the District Council approved plans to build the Mission Room at Green Tye for Mr Richard Hunt with the approval of the Rector and Churchwardens.

Also in 1909 a Housing and Town Planning Act became law. It dealt mainly with the 'housing of the working classes'. The Council discussed whether houses should be built, but responded that: 'there was a want of cottages, but they should not to be built at the expense of the Parish.'

On 2nd June 1910 the death of King Edward VII was reported to the Council.

George V 1910-1936.

In December 1910 there were a large number of rats in the area and there were fears that a plague epidemic was about to break out. In Ware they paid 2d per tail from 6th February 1911 but in Hadham they agreed to a 1d a tail. The fears soon subsided and the bounty was withdrawn in April of the following year.

Mr Crallan

At about this time Mr Crallan is frequently mentioned in the Council minutes. He was an architect who lived at Carldane Court. He had very clever, artistic children who put on the Hadham Follies in the village hall. One of the children was also an architect who designed the two houses to the south of the village hall, North and South Lodge.

Mr Crallan appeared to have been fanatical about motor cars. He was always complaining about the state of the roads and the damage which he claimed resulted to his cars due to inadequate highway maintenance. He is first mentioned on 4 Oct 1910 after he had written a letter complaining of dangerous corners. He requested the District Council to widen the road. The reply stated that this would be done 'only if you bear the costs'.

The other disagreement concerned the water supply. In order to run the water supply from the water works down into the village it had been necessary to enter into agreements to run the pipe across private land. Mr Crallan had agreed to this on condition that he would be allowed free water from taps which were to be used in his 'farmhouse'. It appeared that he was taking an unreasonable amount of water from the system and in particular he used it for washing his cars. Judging by the fuss that was made he must have had a large number of cars.

By August 1912 the disagreement had become so heated that the District Council agreed to ask Mr Crallan if he would accept arbitration by an opinion of Counsel. Mr Crallan attended a Council meeting to discuss the situation 'without prejudice'. He was offered 100,000 gallons a year free, which he refused. The District Council agreed to take the matter to the courts for a decision but then received a petition from the Parish Council supporting Mr Crallan and asking that Mr Minet, a barrister, be appointed as mediator. The District Council 'washed its hands of the whole matter' and passed the decision down to the Parish Council. At the next meeting of the Parish Council, the Councillors couldn't agree on Carldane Court. They sent the problem back to the District with a draft agreement which the District accepted.

Eventually the case was determined in the High Court on 29th and 30th April 1914 by Mr Justice Neville who found that:

'The farmhouse is no longer a farmhouse. It has been turned into a substantial residence. The contract to supply the farmhouse has determined. (Legal word for 'terminated'). Regarding the other part of the contract, to supply a stand-pipe at the farm buildings, the defendant is entitled to a supply but not for washing motor cars'.

The judge awarded partial costs to the Council. Mr Crallan then wrote to the Council giving one month's notice to terminate the contract but the Council replied that it could not depart from the judgement of the High Court.

Mr Crallan had another disagreement with the local authorities. In March 1914 he obtained planning permission to build three cottages in Bromley Road. It appears that he didn't provide proper drainage because it was reported to the Council that 'the sinks have a bucket under, in which waste water runs. Mr. Crallan tells the tenants to throw the waste water on to the gardens. They refuse and let the buckets overflow. The Inspector refuses to issue certificate for occupation and Mr Crallan has given the tenants notice to quit'. These are the cottages which were converted into one dwelling in 1949 and became known as Camber Spring.

Council Houses

In August 1914 the Parish Council set up a committee to look into the provision of Council Houses. The first suggestion was to build six council cottages on land abutting Cox's Lane, or on land at Hadham Cross. The Parish Council preferred the site in Cox Lane, and it was agreed to negotiate with Lord Salisbury who owned the land to purchase three acres at £25 an acre.

The Great War

At the beginning of August the Great War broke out. There are several references in the Parish records to the billeting of troops. The children's home was initially taken over by the War Office as a hospital for patients suffering from typhoid and then as a hospital for the wounded.

Claims were also made against the army for the damage its vehicles were doing to the highway. A claim for the damage done to Camwell Hall Lane was settled at £15 - 10s - 0d.

By April, the Government restricted the outlay of capital on new works and so discussions on the proposed council houses ceased.

On 13th Oct 1915, Zeppelin L16 of the German Naval Airship Division passed over Sawbridgeworth and Much Hadham on its way to deliver an attack on Hertford. There were 9 killed and 15 injured. This was one of the events which helped to foster the malicious rumour that the Dolls who lived at Hadham Towers were spies and that they had a red light on the roof of the house to act as a beacon for raiding Zeppelins. In September 1916, Lt Leefe Robinson shot down a zeppelin over Cuffley for which he was awarded the Victoria Cross. There were more suggestions that German agitators were at work.

At this time there were 350 troops and 20 officers in the village. They were billeted in 93 houses.

There were also prisoners of war in the area who were authorised to work on the land.

In 1918 the Much Hadham Afternoon Women's Institute was formed.

Malting Cottage and the Laurels

Council Houses

As soon as the war was over there were further proposals to build Council Houses. The options were six houses on land which was part of Uffords Farm, six on land the property of Mr Camp, facing Malting Lane, and six on

Cox's Lane. It was resolved to accept the site of one and a half acres at Uffords, Green Tye from Mr Hare for £75. This plan was changed and the District Council decided to build eight cottages, which upset the Parish Council who wanted six only. A contract was let to the Master Builders Association who subcontracted the work to G. L. Thurgood at a price of £7521 - 3s - 6d. The tenant farmer claimed compensation for tenants rights on the land. He claimed that: 'He had ploughed three times and cultivated once'. He was awarded £10 compensation. The houses were ready for occupation by May 1921. Six were let at 7 shillings a week to 'persons of the agricultural labouring class'. and the other two at 10 shillings a week to persons 'not of the agricultural labouring class'.

Water Supply

In Dec 1920 a petition was received from the residents of Dane Bridge Estate for a supply of water. It stated that "the new estate was opened up some 9 or 10 years ago"and was signed by Frederick Pope of Glenside, A C. Sandford of Rayden Cottage, and J H Edwards of Oak Hill Cottage Poultry Farm. After investigation, Mr G L Thurgood reported that to put the Dane Bridge Estate on to water would mean extending the pipe 900 yards. It was suggested that a meeting of the parishioners be convened to discuss the proposal. Nine years later the estate was still without water. A memo signed by Mr C. E. Smith and six other residents on the estate pleaded for a water supply. Mr Thurgood was asked to prepare an estimate to extend the water main to the estate. The estimate was for £400 and the Council resolved that if the petitioners would pay half the cost, the District Council would give the matter favourable consideration. But nothing seems to have come of this because in May 1939 the District Council received yet another letter, this time from E A Golding of Danebridge Lane Association, asking for water supply to Dane Bridge Estate.

War Memorial

The War Memorial was unveiled in January 1921. It is made of Ham Hill stone and was designed by H. Wilson, architect and President of the Arts and Crafts Society. The work was carried out by W. Micklewright of Stoke-under-Haw, Yeovil. The site was given by Captain Montague Norman DSO (later Lord Norman) and it was laid out by G. L. Thurgood and Son who largely employed ex-servicemen to

The War Memorial

do the work. The Memorial which is fifteen feet high stands on a square base and weighs five tons. The Latin Cross is decorated with roses and leaves because an ornamental cross was once looked upon as a symbol of glory. The names of 43 men who fell in the 1st World War are on three of the stone faces of the pedestal. The names of those who were killed in the second World War have since been added. The cost of the memorial was 'upwards of £88'. The service was attended by over six hundred people and the unveiling ceremony carried out by Viscount Hampden. The Clergy who attended were the Rev'd A Tanner - Rector, the Rev'd F Holmes - Curate, the Rev'd J Davies - Congregational Minister, and Father Martin Branagan - R.C. Priest. The Band attended led by the Bandmaster Mr D Roberts.

Buses, Cars and The Railway

The railway was never a financial bonanza for the shareholders, and in 1921 the first bus service was started in Much Hadham. A seven day strike in 1924 started the decline of the railway which was accelerated by the growth in personal car ownership.

Much Hadham Station

The 1920s

In 1923 Mr Roberts applied to the District Council to build six to twelve cottages to let at low rent at Gravel Pit Field at Hadham Cross. (This is the field which is now Ash Meadow and Ferndale). He asked whether he could get the Government's six pound per annum subsidy. He was asked to attend the next Council meeting. He had a letter of support from Mr Topcott but he didn't get the support of the R.D.C..

In 1925 the skeleton of a young girl aged about 17 was found by the new proprietor of The Red Lion in a cavity behind some panelling. There was speculation that the cavity led to a secret staircase. The newspaper report at the time says that 'there was no secret door and no indication that anything else took place here beyond this single concealment of what was probably some sordid village crime'.

In 1927 the Council approved an application from Messrs W Hodge & Son for a petrol pump. In the same year Mr G L Thurgood submitted a plan to convert the old infants school into a cottage. This is now Flint House.

The following year electricity was supplied for the first time to Much Hadham.

The 1930s

In July 1930 it was agreed that six more council houses should be built. The site chosen was in Ducketts Lane, Green Tye. The tender was awarded to Alfred Clark Ltd of Bishop's Stortford. The total cost was £1830. Before work could commence the tenant of the plot, Mr Brace, had to remove his chicken houses. The Council agreed to pay the tithe on the site of the new houses. The houses were complete in November 1931 and were let at 3 shillings and nine pence a week exclusive of rates.

Loss of the Hadham Rural District Council minutes.

The R.D.C. minutes end in January 1931. There should be one more volume but this has been lost.

Braughing Rural District Council

The B.R.D.C. succeeded the Hadham R.D.C. It held its first meeting on 4th April 1935. It combined Buntingford and Hadham R D C's. Because the councillors couldn't agree on a name, they settled for Braughing, roughly halfway between Hadham and Buntingford and with historical connections. One of the Council's first actions was to agree on another Council House scheme, this time for a further eight houses. The vendor of the land was the Rector. The Ecclesiastical Commission attempted to insist on a clause that "nothing shall be done upon the land which may be, or become, a nuisance, annoyance, damage or disturbance to the vendors or to the lessees or persons using the Hut". The B.R.D.C. refused to accept the clause. This development became the Oudle Lane estate. The total cost for the site, including fees was £312 and the ten houses were built by Messrs Thurgood for £3,576 - 0 - 0d. The first tenants for these houses were: F. Gillett, E. Hardy, R. E. Mays, A. E. Sears, W. G. Bayford, J. Copper, A. G. Owers, F. Miles, S. R. Young, and H. W. Bigmore.

Edward VIII 1936

Almost as soon as the Oudle Lane scheme was started there were plans for a further scheme. This time for the Broadfield Way site. The site was owned by Mr Longdon Thurgood. It was 1.136 acres in area and cost £400 inclusive of fees and the redemption of the tithe for £20. These houses were also built by Messrs Thurgood, at a cost of £3,304 - 16 - 0d. They were the first council houses in Hadham to be supplied with gas. The scheme was completed by October 1936. The rents were 3s 9d per week plus rates of 1s 3d per week. The Parish Councillors were upset that they weren't consulted about the tenants. The District Council told them that the houses were built to re-house persons who had been displaced from the unsuitable cottages.

George VI 1936 - 1952

In 1936 Edward VIII abdicated. In the same year a 'Who's Who in Hertfordshire' was published. The following Much Hadham residents were mentioned:

- Aubrey Barker of Manor Cottage,
- E H L Beddington of The Palace,
- W G Bruty of The Lordship,
- Ronald Collet Norman, Chairman of the BBC, son of the late Frederick Henry Norman. Married 1904 to Lady Florence Sibell, daughter of the late 4th Earl of Bradford. Heir, Hugh Ronald Norman, born 1905,
- Rev Maurice Geo. Ponsonby of Much Hadham Rectory. Married the daughter of the late Earl Buxton
- Sir Arnold Talbot Wilson of Wynches. M.P. for Hitchin.

Uninhabitable cottages

Although steps were being taken to provide council houses, many families still lived in appalling condition in tiny cottages with limited facilities. The Council ordered that inspections should be made of cottages where conditions were suspected of being unacceptable and a report should be made stating how they could be improved.

Fire Station

In November 1936 the District Council bought a site owned by Mr R C Norman for a new Fire Station, and plans for its construction were approved in Feb 1937. It was built by Messrs G L Thurgood at a cost of £560-0-0. It was completed by June 1938 and the keys were handed over to the Chief Fire Officer of Much Hadham, Mr Hare. A new Fire Engine was bought in November for £956.

Much Hadham Fire Brigade – About 1942
From top left reading clockwise: Bill Rogers, Jack Groom, Arthur Sayer, Horace Saville, Bert Bigmore, Reg Camp,
Bill Farnham, E. A. (Wopsie) Camp, Jim Biscoe, Bert Hornet, Harry Absolom, Stanley Searle

Council Houses

The District Council bought land at Green Tye for new houses for £16 - 6 - 0 in December 1936 and accepted a tender to build them, and other houses at Allens Green and High Wych, early in the following year. Government approval had to be obtained before building could commence, but the houses were almost ready for occupation by December 1937. They were an additional pair to the Ducketts Lane houses and were allocated to Mr A Tinsley and Mr G Tinsley.

Knowler's nursery

In 1938 Mr Knowler started a nursery in Kettle Green Lane. It was intended for the production of tomatoes and cucumbers which it produced throughout the war. It then transferred to the growing of carnations for a short time and then chrysanthemums. At its peak, it produced two million blooms a year. It has passed into other ownership and now grows lettuces for the supermarkets.

The second World War

War broke out in September 1939 and all meetings of the Council were suspended and local government was to be run by the Emergency Committee. Arrangements were made to camouflage the water towers. The village hall was hired for A.R.P. (Air Raid Precautions) practice at 4s 6d per occasion, once each fortnight for a period of one year, but by 1942 the hall had been taken over for use by the military. The local billeting officer whose job it was to find lodgings for the soldiers was Mr H C Boddington.

Sir Arnold Wilson

When war broke out Sir Arnold Wilson, was living at Wynches. He had been successful in many walks of life. When he graduated from the Royal Military College at Sandhurst he passed out first and was awarded the king's medal and the sword of honour. He then went on to become a successful soldier, explorer, civil administrator, author and politician. His achievements were recognised by the following honours: DSO, CMG, CSI, KCIE and Knight of the Order of St. John of Jerusalem. As the Acting Civil Commissioner in the Persian Gulf he authorised a great number of criminals to be hung. He received a letter from the Foreign Secretary, Lord Curzon, saying that it was His Majesty's Government's policy to show clemency to such people. Wilson sent a contrite reply, but added a P.S.: 'Have hanged another seven this morning'. He was M P for Hitchin from 1933 to 1940. He was a supporter of Hitler and the Fascist movement before the war. When war broke out he made a speech in the House of Commons admitting that he was wrong about Hitler and explained that he had joined the R.A.F. to make amends. He was commissioned as a Pilot Officer and was employed as a rear gunner in bomber aircraft. He was aged 55 at the time. He was shot down over Germany in May 1940 and was killed.

Evacuees

In July 1940, 642 evacuee children arrived in Much Hadham with teachers and helpers.

Henry Moore

One weekend in October 1940 Henry Moore and his wife Irina went to stay with friends, the Labour MP Leonard Matters and his Polish wife, who lived at Fiddlers' Brook, a house in South End. Leonard Matters had always said that if things became too difficult in London the Moores should come and stay with them. When the Moores returned to The Mall studios on the Monday morning they found the studio in ruins. They 'phoned Leonard Matters and returned to Perry Green. Not wishing to outstay their welcome they looked for lodgings in the area and took rooms in Hoglands. In due course

Henry Moore and daughter Mary working in the Hoglands studio

© The Henry Moore Foundation

they bought Hoglands and stayed for the rest of their lives. Moore wrote a letter to a friend on 3rd November 1940 in which he said: 'I've joined the Home Guard here and go out on night duty patrolling the country lanes twice a week. My battledress uniform is very warm, but the trousers are six inches too long and the tunic too tight under the arms. As I was a bayonet instructor for a time in the last war I'm told I shall be asked to instruct our squad in it. But I shall make an awful mess of it. I've forgotten it all.' Henry Moore was a Sergeant.

Henry Moore was already an established artist and was appointed as an official War Artist. His interest in reclining figures was utilised by commissioning him to draw life in the London Underground Stations where Londoners sheltered at night from the bombings. He was also commissioned to visit the coal mines to draw the miners at work in an effort to maintain their morale.

Housing

By the end of 1943 the war in Europe was perceived to be drawing to a close. Attention turned to the provision of improved Council housing stock. A Special Housing Committee was established to identify suitable sites. The site selected is now the Windmill Way estate.

End of the war

In May 1945 the War in Europe was over. The Civil Services were disbanded and anti-gas precautions were relaxed. Many of the private houses were in urgent need of repair but because of shortage of materials Building Certificates had to be obtained before repairs could be undertaken. But plans for the new estate went ahead although there were some difficulties. The owner of Culver objected to the proposed access opposite his house and so an alternative access was provided by purchasing a piece of land at the top of Station Road. The owner of the land was Mrs Clay who objected to the Council's proposals. The revised lay-out plan for the post war housing site embodied an eventual 55 houses instead of the original 36. The site of 8.055 acres was owned by Mr R C Norman and was bought for £60 an acre.

During the war there had been an airfield at Allens Green known as R.A.F. Station Sawbridgeworth. This restricted access to Sawbridgeworth and there was a long delay before the roads were re-opened to the public. After many complaints the road was re-opened in April 1946.

The Ministry of Health wrote to the Council saying that the huts which had formed the army camp at Moor Place were now surplus to requirements, and would the Council wish to convert them for emergency housing purposes? The response was a very curt 'No'.

In September 1946 the cost of maintaining the Rectory had become too expensive and it was sold. Oak Cottage became the new Rectory, but a

The Rectory Lake

bathroom had to be installed to make it habitable. The old Rectory was bought by C. H. Haslam.

By May 1947 Hadham Towers estate was on the market. It became a gravel quarry in the ownership of Messrs Hankin Bros. who traded under the name Sand and Ballast (Hadham) Ltd.

Much Hadham By-pass

After the war the County Council revised its plans for new road construction. It proposed a by-pass around Much Hadham running from a point just north of The Jolly Waggoners across Culver's fields to join up with Danebridge Road by Sidehill House. As with many plans, there was insufficient money to implement the scheme and by the mid-1970s traffic usage had changed so dramatically that the scheme was dropped as being impractical.

Sewage facilities

In 1948 concern was expressed about sewage disposal in the village. The sewage pipes ran into a pit near the river in Dewpits Lane. Discussions took place on whether to hire a bulldozer to construct lagoons on the sewage field or to construct a sedimentation tank, pump and chambers and divert the sewage to the works at the War Department Camp at Wynches. A consulting

The High Street, facing South

engineer was appointed to investigate. Messrs A. Fish and Son of Cobies, High Wych were appointed to excavate 4 lagoons for £168-0-0. This was a success and it was then suggested that separation tanks should be installed. The sewage site was attended by Mr W Ayres. He retired after 28 years service on the grounds of ill health. But the Ministry of Health was becoming concerned about rural water supplies and wrote to the Parish Council in April 1949 asking for information and suggesting consideration of a local enquiry into the arrangements.

Another matter of concern at this time was the proposal to sink a well at Widford for Harlow New Town's water supply against which there was much opposition, but approval was given in April 1950.

The first Tree Preservation Order in Much Hadham under The Town and Country Planning Act was made in March 1951 for the lime trees bordering High Street opposite the Red Lion and two groups of trees in the adjoining paddock. The Palace also changed hands in 1951 and the new owner converted it into separate units.

The Palace

The High Street facing South from the Rose & Crown in the 1950s

© Hertfordshire County Records Office

Elizabeth II   1952

The death of King George the Sixth was reported to the Council on 7th February 1952.

In April 1953 after a review of Petty Sessional Divisions the Court at Much Hadham was abolished. It had sat for over a hundred years.

The evening Women's Institute was formed in 1954.

By March 1955 consulting engineers had been appointed to prepare a scheme for sewage disposal at Much and Little Hadham. An area of land was bought from Mrs Chalk for £60 and a mobile pump was purchased for £209. The proposals to go ahead with a permanent scheme were agreed in December 1957.

1957 appears to have been the year when the deprivations of the war had been left behind and people felt confident and were permitted to undertake private development. An application was approved to change the former Rose and Crown Public House from licensed premises to a private dwelling house for Dr W J Craig. Messrs W Hodge built a new showroom and petrol filling Station, and a new house and garage were approved for Mr G C de Boinville. The architect was Mr P L Hansen Bay, and the house is now known as Nimney Bourne. A hairdressing saloon was also approved for Mr H Ginger.

It seems that in the next year proposals for development had got out of hand. A planning application was lodged for houses to be built on the left hand side of Winding Hill running from the bottom of the hill as far up as a point opposite Danebridge Lane. This was refused, presumably because it was extending the village too far and it was undesirable ribbon development.

After much disagreement and a Public Enquiry, numbers 1 to 4 Malting Lane were demolished in August 1958 under S.25 of The Housing Act as being unfit for human habitation. The land was bought by the brewery for use as a car park for The Old Crown public house.

Old People's Homes.

In Oct 1958 the District Council established a committee to identify suitable sites for old peoples dwellings. Mrs Jean Askwith served on the committee. The intention was to have the dwellings in the centre of villages. It was decided to investigate four villages, which included Much Hadham. In Much Hadham two sites were visited, the first in New Barns Lane. That was considered to be too steep. The second site was in the High Street. It was considered to be ideal except the access to the site was used, late at night, by coaches returning to Hodge's garage and this was considered to be detrimental. Nevertheless it was resolved to provide twelve old peoples homes. The Rev. H. J. Richards of St. Edmund's College representing the owners of the land, agreed to sell some land, provided the scheme fitted in with the owner's own project for future development there.

At this time a number of applications to build houses in Station Road were approved.

Building work continued. The new police house was finished in Malting Lane, and the new telephone exchange. But Hadham Towers which had been used as an office by the gravel company was destroyed so that the gravel beneath it could be extracted.

The 1960s
Broadfield Close

It seems that the District Council rethought its plans for Elderly People's Homes because in 1960 it granted itself planning permission on land which is now Broadfield Close. The plans were changed several times but in 1963 it approved plans for thirteen bungalows plus one dwelling for a warden and then, in 1969 it added the blocks of flats which provided another twelve dwellings.

On 7th September 1965 the last train passed through Hadham before the line closed.

There were eight public houses open in 1965. These were: The Bell, The Old Crown, The Bull, The Jolly Waggoners, The Red Lion in Much Hadham. The White Horse and Prince of Wales were at Green Tye, and the Hoops at

Perry Green. But The Bell converted to a residence a year later and became known as The Old Bell.

In 1968 the Primary school was expanded by adding 5 classrooms, a hall, a kitchen and offices. At that time there was a requirement for the extra space but in subsequent years there were times when the numbers of pupils fell giving fears that the school might close.

Hopleys

Dr David Barker had worked in the village as the general practitioner for most of his life, following in his father's footsteps. He was a keen horticulturist and started 'Hopleys', a nursery garden, in 1968. After he retired from the medical practice he ran the nursery as a full time occupation. The nursery became famous when the potentilla 'Red Ace' was propagated. Hopley's reputation continued to grow as it invariably won medals at the Royal Horticultural Society's Chelsea Flower Show and elsewhere. Hopleys continues to flourish under the management of David Barker's son Aubrey and now has a worldwide reputation.

East Herts District Council

The Local Government Act 1972 changed the structure of local authorities and after a run-in period of a year, East Herts District Council superseded Braughing Rural District Council.

The Rectory, formerly Oak Cottage

© Hertfordshire County Records Office

Michael McAdam

The Rev. Michael McAdam was appointed Rector in December 1973. His previous appointment was as chaplain to the Bishop of London. The living is still in the gift of the Bishop of London but he had recently died, so officially Michael was appointed by Her Majesty the Queen.

Henry Moore

Henry Moore's fame had continued to grow, and as land and property became available he expanded his estate around Hoglands. This gave him the space he required to show his sculpture in the open setting which he preferred. He was also able to sell his work at very high prices, and as a result found that he was paying astronomical levels of income tax. Between 1967 and 1977 he paid £4,350,621 in income tax and in 1975 alone he paid £1,031,275. His advisers explained that if he set up a charitable trust he could use his income in ways which he preferred, so he established initially the Henry Moore Trust but re-organised it later as The Henry Moore Foundation.

On 28th August 1975 John Groom retired as the Postmaster of Much Hadham after 41 years service. He converted the shop to The Old Post House and the Post Office moved to 'The Copper Kettle' at Hadham Cross.

In October 1976, Lordship Cottage became a home for battered wives, but closed after three years and reverted to private residential use.

The Gas Houses

The transfer to North Sea gas from coal gas meant the demise of the gas-works and gas was then piped into the village from outside. The foreman and his wife stayed on in their cottage, but after the foreman died his widow was

John Groom's Post Office

unable to tend the garden and the whole site became overgrown. In 1977 three small houses were built on the site. These were named: The Squash, Scathlan and Bassetts.

Michael O'Connell

Michael O'Connell was a batik artist who designed fabrics for the London stores. He lived in a house which he had built himself next to Henry Moore's property. He was suffering from depression and losing his sight, and was found dead in December 1976. The house passed to his son and was ultimately sold to the Henry Moore Foundation.

First female Fire fighters.

As it became recognised that many women could undertake work alongside men, the Fire Service undertook a recruiting programme to recruit female firefighters. Two of the first female firefighters in the country, Daphne Jordan and Ingrid Kay, joined the Fire Service in 1977 and served alongside the retained fire-fighting crew operating from Much Hadham.

Henry Moore's Sculpture Park

In 1974 Henry Moore's only daughter Mary met Raymond Danowski whom she married shortly after. Henry Moore gave them Minges, an adjacent farmhouse and the agricultural land which surrounded it. Danowski took an interest in Moore's affairs and the Trust which Moore had recently established. In May 1978 Danowski was very much to the fore when a proposal was put forward to create a sculpture park. The scale of the enterprise could be imagined when one heard of the plan to plant 183,000 indigenous trees. The plan was poorly conceived and led to much discontent in the parish. A presentation was made to the noisy and excited villagers in a packed village hall. Several submissions were made to the planning authorities and expensive brochures were distributed marketing the concept, but the idea just faded away.

Church Kneelers

Elizabeth Clarke, Philippa Bagnall, and Evelyn Bruell, embroidered a magnificent set of kneelers for the communion rail in St. Andrew's Church in 1977, followed by others for the choir and return stalls. This triggered a campaign to embroider kneelers for the pews in the nave, and in the next ten years or so, many villagers and friends of the village produced kneelers depicting their chosen subject, thus introducing a mass of colour when the kneelers are displayed for the benefit of visitors.

Roman Catholic Worship

By the kindness of Lt Col and Mrs Hughes-Hallett, a mass centre was started by the Roman Catholics on 2nd March 1939 in an upper room above the garage at The Lordship. There was a congregation of 17. It was still operating in 1954, though the new owners were Mr and Mrs Hill-Wood.

In November 1953 the Catholics acquired the huts near the ford which had been occupied by the Women's Land Army. They obtained planning permission to use the huts as a temporary R. C. Church, church hall and presbytery. In August the following year they were granted a further permission to convert the buildings making them more appropriate to their use.

It seems that as the Roman Catholics raised the money to build their own church, so the price of land increased, thus thwarting their aspirations. A series of events took place which demonstrated that with goodwill the most improbable dreams can come true.

The land which Braughing District Council had acquired to build elderly people's homes had passed to East Herts District Council. Pat Dolan, an enthusiastic and determined Roman Catholic, who wasn't the sort of person to let obstacles stand in his way, had the idea that if the District Council would sell some of the land to the Catholics, they could build some houses and use the profits to build the church.

At about the same time, Dr. Barker the senior partner in the medical practice, retired and he wished to retain in his possession the surgery which he owned. So a part of the newly acquired Catholic land was set aside to build a medical centre. It was built in 1977 at a cost of £36,500 by Brett's the local builders.

Obtaining approval to build the houses was not so easy. The District Council wished to grant permission but the County Council objected as it contravened the County Structure Plan. An appeal was heard and upheld by the Inspector who gave permission to build 36 houses in 1979. These became known as the first phase of Ash Meadow.

The houses were cleverly designed and built by Rialto Ltd., another local builder. Each small house was partnered with its adjacent house to make them look larger and more fitting to the local built environment. It was hoped that they would be bought by local people and a committee was established which could grant a discount to purchasers who had bona fide connections with the village, but even so they were still beyond the reach of the resources of local people.

In 1981 an application was lodged by Rialto to build eighteen two-bedroomed, and three four-bedroomed units, with warden accommodation, a church, a presbytery and caretaker's accommodation. The residential component of this proposal was to enable the less disabled people with epilepsy living at St. Elizabeth's Home to move into the community. The application was refused and an appeal was lodged but owing to the opposition from local people the appeal was withdrawn.

A successful application then followed in 1982 for twelve two-bedroomed and six three-bedroomed, two storey houses, a church, presbytery, and caretakers accommodation. Shortly afterwards permission was granted to demolish the existing Church Hall which had earlier been Land Army Huts and which had served the Roman Catholics since the war as their place of worship.

The building of the Catholic Church complex was started. The Priest's house and the caretaker's house were complete and the building of two sides of the quadrangle leading to the church were then started. Henry Moore had agreed that one of his etchings could be used as a pattern for a stained glass window to be installed in the church. Then a suggestion was put forward that the Catholics might like to share St. Andrew's Church with the Anglicans. In that way it would lessen the expensive burden of maintaining two churches and St. Thomas's at Perry Green. After some discussion an agreement was entered into and the Church has been shared since 1984. The completion of the Catholic Church was abandoned and all evidence of the initial building work was grassed over.

The joint sharing scheme could not have come to fruition without the enthusiastic but careful preparation and negotiations of the Rector. When Michael McAdam was appointed a Canon of St. Albans it was largely in recognition of this achievement.

Page House
Whilst the Catholics were moving ahead with their developments, the District Council built on the remaining part of the land which had originally been bought for Elderly Persons' Homes. The Council built 7 houses, 15 bungalows and 30 units of sheltered accommodation with a wardens house. The road leading to the development was named Ferndale. The sheltered accommodation, which was built in 1984, was named 'Page House' in memory of Charlie Page, the last blacksmith to work in Much Hadham, and father of Jean Page the Parish Council Chairman.

Water Cress
When the railway served Much Hadham, there were a number of water cress beds alongside the River Ash owned and managed by the Ginger family. At one time a waggon load a day of water cress went into London to serve the lucrative hotel trade. In 1980 the Ginger's water cress fields were sold and

were converted to a fish farm.

In the same year the postal sorting service was abandoned in Much Hadham and transferred to Ware.

St. Elizabeth's

In 1980 work started on a new school building at St. Elizabeth's. The school and home has developed since it was founded in 1902. It continues to expand as standards improve both educationally and domestically. The residents now live in comfortable, bright surroundings far different from the early days, but with the same loving care and attention provided by the Daughters of the Cross.

The Hall

The Hall was put up for sale by Richard de la Mare the son of Walter de la Mare in the autumn of 1980. It has been suggested that Walter wrote some of his poetry in the garden of The Hall. The contents of the house were sold and attracted a large gathering over several days. The contents included Japanese pottery, porcelain and lacquer ware. There were also European ceramics and glass and an extensive library, plus watercolours, prints and oil paintings, furniture, works of art and clocks.

The Hall in the 1950s

The Hall remained unsold for some time. The new owner claimed that the roof was in such a poor state that he couldn't afford to repair it. After considerable negotiations he was given planning permission to build two houses in the grounds provided he used the profits to repair the roof. Those two houses are now called Lowfield House and Newtons.

Culver

Harry Sporborg, a merchant banker, had lived at Culver for some years. The field opposite Culver's frontage faced the Windmill Way estate. When the Sporborgs decided to move away in the early 1980s they applied for planning permissions on some of their surrounding garden land. Their proposals were refused but were taken to appeal which was partly upheld. They were given permission to build two bungalows to the north of Culver in the kitchen garden opposite Broadfield Way. This land was sold on several times and each purchaser applied to build slightly larger dwellings. The final permission was granted in 1983 and the two houses Grays and Willows were built. Harry Sporborg also offered the field to the west of Culver to the District Council at a reasonable price which the Council accepted. The District Council was then able to construct an improved access into Windmill Way making it easier for the residents to reach the village centre.

Culver changed hands again in 1987. It was on the market for some time and was eventually bought by a developer. He converted the coach house, the stables and all the other outhouses into residences and some further derelict stables into industrial units.

Walnut Close

Between 1983 and 1984 planning permission was given to build six houses to the north of Yew Tree and Holy Oak Cottages at Hadham Cross. These are now known as Walnut Close.

Decline in shopping facilities.

In the last twenty years there has been a general decline in the number of shops in the village. In 1978 Careless the ironmonger closed down. Alterations were made to the building and it re-opened as Careless Antiques. It provides an authentic setting for the occasional television programme.

Peter Ginger's hairdressing saloon was rebuilt as a house now called Tanglewood.

Swain's the butchers closed in 1990 and after several attempts gained planning permission to open as a Spar mini-market and hairdressers. This replaced the more traditional village shop, which had traded on the corner at Hadham Cross as Luck's, Jennings', Quinn's, and Carter's throughout its long life.

Chamberlain's antique shop closed, and as the the building was in such a poor state a new house replaced it in 1986, but kept the same name.

Stansted Airport

After a long public enquiry the Government gave approval for Stansted Airport to build a new terminal and expand as London's third airport in June 1985. Speculators homed in on the area and bought options on large areas of land in the vicinity of the airport, but the planners confined the development to the peripheries of the larger towns, in particular Bishop's Stortford. Nevertheless the increased traffic volumes and aircraft noise have been harmful to the village, and the western boundary of Bishop's Stortford has moved considerably nearer to the village.

The Old Railway Station - Miller's View.

British Rail was refused planning permission to convert the old railway station into residential units and to build additional houses in 1967. The station then fell into a state of neglect.

In 1970 the District Council decided to acquire the land by means of a Compulsory Purchase Order, in order to build garages for the residents of Windmill Way, but the Council never proceeded with the idea.

The station yard remained in use as a coal yard for Simmons and Taylor who built themselves a new office in 1978. But they only stayed until 1982 when they moved their entire operation to the old Widford Station site.

Because the Much Hadham station site was unused it became open to abuse. It was a convenient place to dump rubbish. Young men with motor cycles used it as a field trials circuit, and it was settled on by 'travellers' for a time. In the end the complaints prompted the Parish Council to ask British Rail to do something constructive with the site.

There were only two options, either industrial or residential use. British Rail Property Board obtained outline planning permission for residential use in February 1987 and sold the site to Buckle Limited who built ten detached houses in 1988 which they called Miller's View in recognition of the windmill which once stood there. Buckles' application for another 7 detached houses further northward was refused, and although an appeal was lodged, it was withdrawn before the appeal was heard.

The development of Millers View was not without controversy. The developers claimed that the pigs which the Mundays, the neighbouring farmers, kept in the adjoining field were prejudicial to their development. The dispute went to the High Court and the Mundays won the day.

The Grounds of the Henry Moore Foundation

Death of Henry Moore

Henry Moore died on the 31st August 1986, aged 88. He had lived in Perry Green for 45 years. Mrs Moore died on the 9th April 1989. They are both buried in St. Thomas' churchyard. The Headquarters of the Henry Moore Foundation remains at Perry Green where it continues to fulfil Moore's wishes 'to advance the education of the public by the promotion of their appreciation of the fine arts and in particular the works of Henry Moore'.

The Forge Museum

Miss Jean Page's family had worked the forge for several generations. In 1990 she arranged to hand over her property to the Hertfordshire Building Preservation Trust. They renovated the buildings and created a museum. The forge remains as a working forge but does not shoe horses, and the garden has been laid out as a typical Victorian garden.

The Henry Moore Foundation

The Henry Moore Foundation made a further attempt to improve its facilities at Perry Green. The concept was primarily the brainchild of the Foundation's Director Sir Alan Bowness. It comprised three separate components. The first was to build a reception centre linking the main building at Dane Tree House with the adjacent buildings plus considerable extensions. The second was to erect a new Study Centre with a Print and Drawing Gallery, and the third was to demolish an existing barn and replace it with a Sculpture Gallery. There was considerable local opposition and all three applications were refused. The Foundation appealed against the decision on the Reception Centre and the Study Centre and a Public Enquiry was held in the village hall. Although the Inspector was favourably inclined towards the development he dismissed the appeal on the grounds of difficulty of access through the local narrow lanes.

The Upper Vestry

Two churchwardens are elected each year. One of them is responsible for the fabric of the church. Penelope Wrong took up this post in 1991 and under her vigorous leadership a number of improvements to the church were undertaken. In 1993 an additional floor was introduced into the vestry which utilised the existing space far more effectively. Other improvements were introduced at the same time including the provision of lavatories. The upper vestry can now be used for the Sunday School and for coffee after church and other small gatherings.

Moor Place in the 1950s

Mark Norman and the Henry Moore Memorial Window

Mark Norman, who had been the benevolent leader and counsellor to the village from his home at Moor Place died on the 13th December 1994. Plans were already in hand to install the Henry Moore stained glass window into St. Andrew's Church. It was originally intended to place it in the Roman Catholic Church. Penelope Wrong, Mark Norman's daughter, was the main organiser in her position as church warden. Many members of Mark Norman's family, a number of whom live in the United States of America, were generous contributors towards the expenses. The window called 'The Tree of Life' was dedicated by the Rt. Reverend Lord Runcie, a past Archbishop of Canterbury, on the 30th July 1995. The Roman Catholic Bishop James O'Brien, Bishop in Hertfordshire was in attendance. The window was made by Patrick Reyntiens and his son John. The church was packed to overflowing although many extra seats had been provided for the occasion. It was a farewell appearance for Canon Michael McAdam who retired the following day after nearly twenty one years in office.

Close of Hadham Towers waste disposal site
The last load of waste was delivered to the Hadham Towers site on 23rd October 1995. The site will be covered with topsoil and landscaped to its original contours.

Epilogue
I have tried to take the reader through the history of our parish by covering the major events without commenting on the rights or wrongs of the different aspects. I expect that I have omitted some important points, though this is not intentional. In the early years, much of our history depended on the activities of the church and state. It is interesting to observe how we appear to have become more ordinary as the years progressed. The key event appears to have been the bequest of Queen Ethelfleda of her lands to the Bishops of London over one thousand years ago. Who can imagine what the village will look like in another thousand years or even a hundred?